PLAY WITH US!

Freya Jaffke

Play with Us!

Social Games for Young Children

Translated by Nina Kuettel
Illustrated by Christiane Lesch

WECAN
WALDORF EARLY CHILDHOOD
ASSOCIATION OF NORTH AMERICA

Play With Us!
First English Edition
© 2016 Waldorf Early Childhood Association of North America
ISBN: 978-1-936849-33-8

Originally published in German as
Spiel mit uns!
Verlag Freies Geistesleben, Stuttgart
The text is taken from the fourth edition (2007),
the illustrations from the first edition (1990).

Published in the United States by the
Waldorf Early Childhood Association of North America
285 Hungry Hollow Road
Spring Valley, NY 10977
www.waldorfearlychildhood.org

Visit our online store at
store.waldorfearlychildhood.org

This publication is made possible through a grant from the Waldorf Curriculum Fund.

Contents

Preface to the Fourth Edition

The latest editions of this book have mainly focused on outdoor games. Such games counteract the much-lamented lack of movement present in today's early childhood programs, and address deficits in beginning schoolchildren's physical dexterity and agility. Bringing these games to children does not have so much to do with special training as it does with offering children opportunities for a wide variety of movement and the possibility of becoming more dexterous through play.

Parents and educators are equally called upon to make sure children have opportunities for the lively development of free yet focused movement. The simplest materials, such as balls, ropes, boards, stilts and, of course, simply enjoying a walk, are much more valuable than being strapped into a play car with its monotonous, mechanical motion.

At the end of the first major developmental phase of childhood, around age six or seven, children are able to guide and control their own movements, meaning they feel comfortable in their own bodies, and are able to bring with them the best preconditions for attentiveness and joy in learning at school.

For everyone who has anything to do with children, may these simple games encourage a higher level of attention to lighthearted, fun play.

Freya Jaffke
October, 2006

Preface to the First Edition

The games that have been compiled here are not new. They are tried-and-true, harmless, fun children's games. The impetus to compile them together with new descriptions came about because of impressions I received from many different places. Preschool-age children are either confronted with too many strict rules for games or they are too strongly awakened and challenged on an intellectual level. Sometimes, because of choosing the wrong game or being limited to one kind of game, children are limited in their natural enjoyment of movement or prevented from participation in games appropriate to their age group.

Most of the games can be played spontaneously, without a great deal of preparation, anywhere groups of children are gathered. However, one condition for success is that the adult leading the group is very familiar with how the games are played and knows the lyrics and melodies for the songs. He or she should make an effort at pleasant, calm, characteristic gestures of play when required and also invent imaginative variations that arise out of the unique circumstances of each play group. This is how to create real joy in play.

Free, imaginative play is most significant for preschoolers' development. Along with this, there are always those empty moments in the life of a child, at home or in kindergarten, when a game with other children can be a harmonious, happy way to fill some time. One should carefully choose only a few games that are played repeatedly instead of overwhelming the children with a whole array of games. Children quickly catch on to a game and integrate it into their free play as a matter of course, especially when they are around age seven.

With most of the games presented here, additional paragraphs offer rules in case older children are playing. Naturally, the rules can be changed or varied to suit the unique situation in each group.

Only those games that have stood the test of time and have proven to be successful in practice are included. Songs that have pentatonic melodies, or fifth-tone scale melodies, are preferable to other perhaps better-known melodies since they are more appropriate for a preschooler's stage of development. Handled correctly, they have a refreshing and cheering effect.

May this book find its way into many nurseries and kindergartens and contribute to young children being able to take part in social games that are appropriate for their age group.

I would like to express my heartfelt gratitude to all the colleagues and parents of kindergartners who helped with this book.

Freya Jaffke
December, 1989

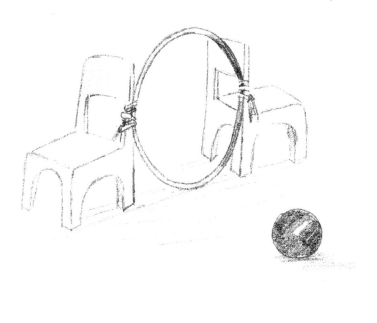

Indoor Games

Introduction

The following indoor games can be played on the most varied of occasions. Some are especially suitable during waiting times at the doctor's office or train station; for example, "Rinky Red," "I See Something You Don't See," or "Hide the Nut." These games may even be played with just one child.

The guessing games should be carefully chosen and not played too often or too long so that children do not become overtired. If one chooses hiding games, such as "Hide the Nut" or "From Mother Bird" for a mixed-age group where the children know each other very well, one will always discover that the six-year-olds interact with the three- and four-year-olds with great patience and tolerance. Not only do they choose easy hiding places, they are also tactfully helpful during the search. The same is true for many of the guessing games.

Games involving the use of a blindfold have been consciously left out of this collection. A preschool-age child still lives very closely connected with the environment through all of the physical senses. This connection should not be disturbed too early; also, a young child's ability to imagine the surroundings is not yet strong enough to maintain orientation while wearing a blindfold. Anxiety and insecurity are very natural reactions and therefore such games are better left for children of school age.

Circle games may of course be included in the selection of indoor games. A good example is "Kling, Klang, Gloria" (see p. 47), which can naturally also be played outdoors in the yard.

More circle games can be found in the book *Tanzt und singt!* ("Let's Dance and Sing," Verlag Freies Geistesleben, 2003; English edition forthcoming from WECAN).

Rinky Red

Folk Song

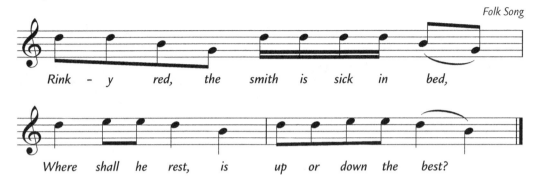

Rink - y red, the smith is sick in bed,

Where shall he rest, is up or down the best?

The children sit in a loose group or circle. An adult or child has hidden a nut, or something else, in one fist.

Stack your fists one on top of the other and tap them together while singing the above song. After the song one child has to guess which fist contains the nut by pointing to it. If the guess is correct, we open our hand and say:

That's right, that's right, you are so bright.

If the empty fist was picked, we show our empty hand and say:

Sadly, Mr. Bloom is not in this room.

At the same time we open the correct hand to show the child the nut is there.

If, by chance, you have a smaller group of children who are all over six years old, you can let each child have a second turn if the first guess is wrong and say the corresponding rhyme only after the second guess.

This little game can be played anywhere. It helps to pass the time in waiting rooms and is also a good way to provide a distraction for children. You can use any small object that will fit in your fist such as a small rock, a finger ring, a wad of paper, etc.

I Went Fishing

The children sit around a table with their hands outstretched and lying flat on the table. The adult is the first fisher and then each child gets a turn as the fisher. The fisher glides one hand above the children's outstretched hands and says:

I went fishing,
I went fishing,
All night long, just like I ought,
But not one fish have I yet caught.

With the word "caught" everyone quickly pulls their hands back and the fisher tries to tap one hand. If she touches a hand that means she caught a fish. Whether or not the first "fishing expedition" was "successful" the fisher can try once or twice more before it is another child's turn.

If the children are five or older, one child is the fisher until all, or almost all, of the fish are caught. That means every hand that is touched has to be removed from the table. When there is only one hand remaining on the table, that child gets to be the next fisher.

With the older children you have to pay careful attention that they do not pull their hands away too quickly, before the word "caught" has been said. In a mixed-age group, if the game is played as described above, you will have to be very lenient in this regard.

Little Mouse

A group of children sit around a table on which are scattered a handful of buttons (naturally, other objects would work too, such as colorful rocks or small sea shells.) One child closes his eyes while another child points to one specific button. The first child opens his eyes and begins to carefully slide one button after the other closer to him. If he comes to the button that the other child pointed out, everyone cheerfully shouts:

Hooray, Little Mouse has come to stay!

All the buttons are put back in the middle of the table and the game begins again.

This is a game in which all the merriment and excitement of shouting "hooray!" always leads back again to rapt attention and silence.

I See Something You Don't See

An adult or older child (age four or five) picks out an object and says: "I see something you don't see and it is [for example] blue."

The others name everything they see around them or on them that is blue for as long as it takes to find the right object. The one who named it may now choose another object. If the same child keeps naming the right object, then the adult should choose another child to continue the game.

This game can be played anywhere. It is especially well-suited for times when short waiting periods are involved, such as at the doctor's office. You should just make sure that the chosen object can really be seen by all the participants and has not perhaps been imagined. Six-year-olds, who already possess some powers of imagination, sometimes will choose something that is in the next room, although without consciously trying to break the rules.

If this game is played with six- to nine-year-olds you can take it a step further and say:

"I see something you don't see, and it is blue and in the hallway" (or in another room that is very familiar to everyone).

Magic, Magic, Abracadabra

All the children sit in a circle. Playing the magician, an adult goes around the circle touching each child's head, and says:

Magic, magic, abracadabra
Black cats, one, two, three,
This is what you shall be:
A bird! [for example]

The magician and the enchanted ones then all fly around in a circle for the duration of an applicable song or verse. Then the magician says:

When I say,
All the birds must fly away.

Everyone returns to his or her place and the game begins again.

Older children really enjoy playing the magician. Of course, the adult joins in with the songs and verses, and also whispers in the magician's ear what spell should be cast because it has to be something that applies to a familiar song or verse.

The chosen child could also be a different animal or someone who practices a certain trade or craft.

Happily Our Kernel Wanders

Melody: Freya Jaffke

Hap - pi - ly our ker - nel wan - ders, In - to the lit - tle boat, up and un - der,

Quick and qui - et jump in - side, But tell no child where you hide.

The children sit either in a circle, on a bench or next to each other on the grass. Hands are in laps with palms together in the shape of a boat.

An adult (or one of the children) has a small kernel in her folded hands (for example, a plum or cherry pit, or even a small rock). While singing the song above, she goes from one child to the next and touches the slightly open "boats" with her hands.

She inconspicuously lets the kernel fall into one of the boats. When the song is finished, a child is chosen to guess where the kernel is by saying the following counting verse (just like eeny-meeny-miney-mo):

Child, my dearest, please do tell,
Where does the kernel hide so well?

You may also dispense with the counting verse and simply choose one child to make a guess.

In a mixed-age kindergarten class the child doing the guessing is always given the kernel, even if she has not found it by the third try. She is then the next child to let the little kernel wander. If the children are between the ages of six and nine, the counting verse should always be used. If the kernel has not been found by the third try, then the child who has the kernel in her hands is the next one to let it wander.

There Once Were Some People Who Fell in a Well

The children sit in a circle. An adult chooses a few children to sit in the middle of the circle and play "the people." An adult says:

There once were some people
Who fell in a well.
Who can pull them out again?

The adult makes an immediate suggestion and says, for example:

Surely the violinist can.

Then he plays a tune and everyone imitates playing the violin. Afterward he picks children from the circle, the same in number as are in the well. Each child from the circle pulls out one person from the well and takes them back to their place. Then it is that child's turn to go to the middle of the circle and sit on the floor for the game to begin again.

Children who are older than five are often able to make suggestions of their own for typical occupations or activities. Instead of songs, you might rather choose verses that have to do with different types of handiwork or trades accompanied by the typical gestures of movement associated with the activity. If the game is played with first or second graders, you could have just one man or woman fall into the well. When pulling the person out of the well you would say [for example]: "Who is the best violin player?"

The Cobbler

This game should only be played with a group of children who know each other very well.

The children sit in a circle. One child sits on a chair in the middle of the circle (the "cobbler") and keeps her eyes closed. The following is either sung or spoken:

In a cellar, dark and dreary,
Lives a cobbler, poor and weary,
He has no light, he has no light,
There, dear Sun does not shine bright.

Now an adult signals for one child to come and stand behind the cobbler, lightly tap him or her on the shoulder and ask:

Cobbler, are my shoes finished?

The cobbler answers [for example], "Yes, Molly!"

This game requires presence of mind and a lot of empathy from adults. If you notice that a child playing the cobbler hesitates to guess who is standing behind her, you should go to her and gently turn her head a little toward the child standing behind her and say: "Yes, Molly."

It is best to only let children who are more than four-and-a-half to five years old play the cobbler.

Tap, Tap, Little Hammer

The following game is very similar to the cobbler game.

An adult nods to one child sitting in the circle to come over and stand in front of her. The child covers his eyes with his hands and lays his head in the adult's lap. The adult nods to another child to come over. The second child stands behind the first child, gently taps him on the back and says:

Tap, tap little hammer.

The first child has to guess who was knocking. If he hesitates, it is all right to let him take a peek, and the adult says something like: "That's Justine, right?"

Now the child who knocked gets a turn at closing her eyes and the game continues.

This game is only possible with children who know each other very well. It is too challenging for children less than four years of age. Five- and six-year-olds will often one day happily whisper to an adult: "I can tell who is knocking by the sound of their voice!"

I Have a Little Bell

Melody: Freya Jaffke

I have a lit-tle bell, a shi-ning sil-ver bell,

Kling-a-ling-a-ling, kling-a-ling-a-ling, This bell I shall to [An-na] bring.

One of the children sitting in a circle is given a small bell. She walks around the middle of the circle singing "I Have a Little Bell."

The child named in the song cups his or her hands and the bell is placed there. Now this child may go around the circle, and so it continues. An adult should always choose the name of the child who gets the bell.

This game is especially well-suited for a new class where the children do not yet know each other very well. Naturally, children who hesitate or make a gesture indicating they do not wish to have a turn will not be forced. In that case you would simply repeat the last line with a different name. It may be necessary for an adult or an older child to accompany three-year-old children around the circle.

A variation for children over five years old is as follows. One child keeps her eyes closed. All the other children have their hands behind their back. One child is quietly given the bell. The children sing the following:

I have a little bell,
A shining silver bell,
Kling-a-ling-a-ling, kling-a-ling-a-ling,
Now can you guess who has the thing?

When the song begins, the first child opens her eyes and waits for the child with the bell behind his back to ring it during the last line of the song. If she guesses who has the bell, she may then give the bell to another child. If she is not right, the child with the bell may pass it on to someone else.

My Little House Is Bare

A number of chairs are arranged in a circle with one more chair than there are children present. One of the two children sitting on either side of the empty chair may put her hand on the chair and, after the song is finished (which may only be sung in a fifth), she may ask one of the other children to come sit in the empty chair:

My little house is bare,
I wish for Simon to come here.

With this game we have to be careful that the same child is not asked over and over. If three-year-old children are also in the circle, then we may have to gently sing out a name for them when it is their turn to wish for someone.

School children between seven and nine years old still like to play this game. Under certain circumstances, they may make it more challenging by giving themselves names of flowers. Then it would go something like:

My little house is bare,
I wish for Tulip to come here.

Naturally, with this variation the circle should not be too large because that would make it difficult to come up with enough flower names.

Bello, Your Bone Is Gone

The children sit in a circle. One of the older children lies rolled up on the floor like a dog ("Bello"), with face in hands and eyes closed. The "bone" (a piece of round wood) is lying in front of him. Another child quietly sneaks up to Bello, takes the bone and hides it behind her back. As soon as all the children have their hands behind their backs, they all say together:

Bello, your bone is gone without a trace,
Look around for its hiding place!

Now Bello goes around and tries to find out who has the bone. The child with the bone gets to be Bello the next time.

One of Us Is Missing

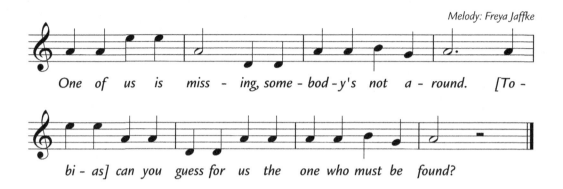

Melody: Freya Jaffke

One of us is miss-ing, some-bod-y's not a-round. [To-bi-as] can you guess for us the one who must be found?

The children sit in a circle. One child (not younger than five) closes her eyes and puts her head on her knees. An adult signals another child to come over and hide under a large cloth in front of the adult. When the song begins, the first child looks around the circle and tries to discover who is missing, but she must wait until the song is finished to name the missing child.

If you see that a child is having difficulty, begin raising the cloth in front of the hidden child a little at a time until he or she is recognized. To make the guessing much more challenging for children between seven and nine years of age, as soon as one child is hidden, all the others quickly switch seats.

24

Knick, Knack, Knead

The children sit in a circle. Each child is holding a string that has been knotted into a circle (the knot has to be very small). A wooden bead has been threaded onto one of the strings and one child has it hidden in his hand. Everyone begins moving their hands one against the other and over to their neighbor while the bead is being passed from one hand to the next around the circle.

One child (not less than five years old) stands in the middle of the circle, observes the moving hands and tries to tell in whose hands the bead has landed at the end of the verse.

Knick, knack, knead,
Run, you colorful bead,
Run and run, do not slow,
Without rest you have to go.
Knick, knack, knead,
Hide, you colorful bead.

With kindergartners, after one or two false guesses, the child holding the bead will open his hand. Then another child may stand in the middle.

This game is suitable for children no younger than age five. With schoolchildren in grades 1-3 the child standing in the middle will be replaced by the child left holding the bead. If the bead has not been found after three guesses, an adult will choose another child to stand in the middle of the circle.

Hide the Nut

The children sit in a large circle. One child keeps her eyes closed. Now an adult hides the nut (any smaller object will do) on one of the other children; perhaps on the tip of his slipper, on top of his head, in the clasp of his suspenders, on his shoulder, or half-visible in the front pocket of his overalls. Then the adult says: "Come on!" and the "seeker" opens her eyes and begins slowly walking around looking at each child and trying to find the nut. You might say something like: "warm, warmer," and when she is very close, "hot!"

As soon as the nut is discovered, another one is hidden for the next child, and so on.

While often an adult will have to hold the hand of a three or four-year-old while searching for the nut, the five- and six-year-olds like to demand "really hard hiding places." The more difficult hiding places should be outside of the circle somewhere in the room. You might initially indicate the right direction to search, but then let the child react to directives of "cold" or "colder" and "warm," "warmer" and "hot." Children find the greatest pleasure in the search.

From Mother Bird

An adult sits on a stool (the nest) as the mother bird. Next to her sits a child, or an adult, as the father bird. The children sit all around them on the floor; they are all little birds. As soon as it is very quiet, the mother bird puts her face in her hands and goes to sleep. All the little birds immediately fly off and hide in agreed-upon places. It is recommended that an adult help the children find suitable hiding places. After everyone has found a good hiding place, father bird awakens mother bird and she begins searching for all the little birds. All the bird children who have been found then fly with their mother and help in the search for the others. Then they all return to the nest and the game begins again.

It is especially fun if once in a while mother bird flies off to a hiding place and all the young birds have to close their eyes and then set out on the search together.

If there happen to be several parents taking part in the game, they are all mother birds, but each is only allowed to discover his or her own child's hiding place; they must ignore all the other children. The same goes for when the bird children are searching; each child searches until his or her own mother or father is discovered.

Outdoor Games

Introduction

We try to arrange outdoor play in such a way that the children are able to use their imagination and creative energy in a variety of ways. Above all, it is in the sandbox that children of all ages quickly find play activities suited to their age group.

If we provide enough logs, boards, play cloths and string, the all-important creative play has no limits and the children are able to realize their new ideas each day.

The fact that children will always try to build onto or remodel even permanent structures like a garden shed is a testament to their tireless, internally-driven creative activity.

Naturally, things like balls, jump ropes, hoops, "horse reins," and stilts belong in our store of outdoor playthings. Using these things helps train children's motor skills, and children love using them. Adults need not be consciously trained to guide children and help with the widely recognized problem of developmental deficits among children just beginning school.

Other opportunities for play in the yard, or on a walk in the park or forest, include various social games, which are presented here with mixed-age groups in mind (from three to seven years old). These games are very easy to play while being neither too challenging nor too boring for children.

We always try to consider the different behavioral aspects of young children from various age groups when playing these social games. We must take great care to patiently guide the three- and four-year-olds while requiring a little more exactness from the five- and six-year-olds in following the agreed-upon rules. For instance, in the call-and-catch game "All My Little Children" (see p. 38) we have to make sure that the "fox" really waits until the end of the calling-song before he starts running. At the same time, we would never make a three- or four-year-old who had initially joined the "mother" go back just because she decided to run off with the other "foxes" and "children," tried to catch another child when she wasn't the "fox" or allowed herself to be caught when she was the "fox." Such behavior has its place in a mixed-age group; it is absolutely no problem. As a matter of fact, the older children will imitate the adults' alert, benevolent tolerance toward the younger children.

The simplest thing is to just begin with some social games, without having to organize very much, just playing with the children who happen to be standing around us, or with a group of children who ask to play a game. Other children will quickly join in, but some may continue to play quietly and happily by themselves under a bush or tree.

On windy days, when children are compelled to run and jump, running and tag games are very appropriate. The simple way these games are played allows children to relish all their joy and happiness in movement and yet the needed structure is still there.

Children who easily cross the line from joyful play to yanking or roughhousing, during tag for example, will be reminded about the rules we agreed on (for example, during tag to only touch a child and then let them go again). Sometimes it may be necessary to take the child by the hand. He or she will usually get back into the game after only a short pause to think about what happened.

If we have a group made up of only six-year-olds, we are always careful that the agreed-upon rules are followed. This is the age when children give themselves rules for play and also like to imaginatively change established rules, but everyone will accept the agreed-upon rules.

In the following, games with a more prominent social element are presented first, followed by the games that are especially helpful for development of motor skills. Lastly, there are the little games that are appropriate for children's parties.

We Come Here from a Far-off Land

Melody: Freya Jaffke

We come here from a far-off land, and we are walk-ing hand in hand, We glad-ly come when bid - den; Our work is safe-ly hid - den.

Two rows of children stand facing each other a good distance apart. If it is a mixed-age group of three to six-year-olds, the five- and six-year-olds may form a row and the younger children will form a row opposite, with adults included.

The children in row A think of an activity that is easy to express through miming gestures. For example: Sawing, rocking a baby, polishing shoes, sewing, kneading dough, or picking flowers. Now the children hold hands and sing the above song while walking towards the children in row B.

When the two rows are close together, there is the following dialogue:

B: *What kind of people are you?*
A: *Very honest people, [everyone bows]*
From the back, [everyone turns around and bows again]
And the front. [everyone bows again toward the front]
B: *Show us your work!*

The children in Row A do their miming gestures as long as it takes Row B to guess what they are doing. Then they quickly run back and the children in Row B try to tag them. Afterward everyone returns to his or her row and the game begins anew, but now the other row has to think of an activity.

33

If this game is played with schoolchildren in the first grade and up, then you should start with two rows that are approximately equal. The children who are tagged have to join the other row. After the game is over, the row with the most children wins.

However, that much change during the game would be irritating for kindergartners. They are best able to keep track of things and have a sense of security when they have to always return to their respective rows, the younger children to the adults and the five- and six-year-olds to their own row. The fun of miming the activities and guessing what they are far outweighs any comprehension of winning or losing the game. If they are allowed to stay together as a group, the five- to seven-year-olds develop the miming gestures with tremendous zeal and imagination. Often they will not be content with miming only one activity, such as sawing or sewing, but will imitate a whole sequence of activities. For instance, they may begin with giving baby a bath, then diapering the baby, then rocking the baby; or picking flowers, filling a vase with water, and sticking the flowers in the vase.

This way the guessing is made all the more difficult. The six-year-olds' happiness increases even more if the adults in the row opposite take a long time to guess what they are doing.

Bridge of Gold

Melody: Ch. Jahr

Bridge of gold, oh gold-en bridge, now who has bro-ken you? The
gold - smith, the gold - smith, and his young daught-er too.
Go a - cross; Go a - cross; the last one we will
cap - ture with sticks and spears and laugh - ter.

Two older children stand opposite one another and form a gate with their hands and arms. Quietly, so the others do not hear, you agree which one will be the "Sun" and which one will be the "Moon."

The other children form a line in single file and, led by an adult, walk through the gate and continue walking around the bridge and through the gate in a figure eight while singing the above song. At the end of the song, with the words "sticks and spears and laughter," the bridge children lower their arms and capture the child standing on the bridge.

The captured child is asked: "Do you want Sun or Moon?"

If he says "Sun" then he must stand behind the bridge-child who is the "Sun" and the game begins again.

After all the children are captured, it has to be decided which row of children are going to be "devils" and which are going to be "angels." A counting verse could be helpful.

Or, the adult could present both hands to one of the bridge-children. In one fist is hidden a small rock, for instance, and the child must choose. If she chooses the fist with the rock then all the children standing behind her are "devils" and the other row are the "angels."

Now, first the row of "angels" are cradled (best by two adults) by the child lying across the adult's outstretched, clasped arms. The following verse is spoken very rhythmically:

Angel, angel, heavy laden,
With so much silver and gold;
High in Heaven,
High in Heaven,
And back to the Earth below.

The child is set back on the ground with the last line of the verse.

36

Next, one of the "devils" stands between the adults' locked arms and is carefully and rhythmically pushed forward and back with the following verse:

A devil is rolled, rattled and shaken,
Right out of the house he's [or she's] taken!

If this game is played with a mixed-age group that includes three-year-olds, they may leave the waiting line because often they are not yet able to stand in line and wait until everyone is captured. We should just let them do as they please in this regard. It does not bother the older children if a younger one leaves for a while to go play something else. If you have a large group of children, you may decide to have two children captured at once.

Experience has shown that the shaking and rattling of the "devil" is so popular that the children will often get in line again to be "shaken," even the ones who were "angels."

All My Little Children, Come To Me!

Melody: Freya Jaffke

MOTHER: All my lit-tle child-ren, come to me! CHILDREN: Oh, no, we can't! MOTHER: Why e - ver not? CHILDREN: The fox is here! MOTHER: All my lit - tle child - ren come to me!

The goose-mother stands in the yard, playground or meadow with all her goose-children opposite her, a little distance away. The fox stands to the side by a tree or some other designated place. It is advisable to always have a group of children at all three places and not individual children. The game begins with the singing dialogue above.

After the dialogue, all the "children" run over to their "mother" and the "fox" tries to catch them before they get there. However, the fox only tags them and then lets them run off.

If an adult happens to be in the group of "children," then the "foxes" really love to try and catch the adult.

Now, the children ask again what role they can play and in most cases it will work out that everyone gets to be what they want, even if it means that an adult is the only one left on the "children's" side.

If you are playing this game for the first time but without a second adult present, then you just say the verse for the opposite groups and they will repeat it.

Chase and Catch

On cool, windy days when it is difficult for children to concentrate on play in the sandbox or yard the game of chase and catch is a favorite activity. If we are unable to play in our own yard but are perhaps able to go to a park with a spacious lawn, the first thing to do is show the children where the boundaries are all around.

It's important that children between three and six years old are able to participate in the game in accordance with their age, without any kind of formality or much attention to the rules.

1. An adult names one of the older children; all the others run after him and try to catch him. If they are successful, another child is named, and so on. It is cause for great joy if the adult names herself once in a while.

2. Two children of about equal strength are named and they try to catch each other. The other children remain standing with an adult and watch the game. It is advisable to not allow more than three pairs of children to play at once because both the onlookers and the players can easily lose track of who is chasing whom.

3. An adult names a nearby goal; a path or sidewalk bordering the grass, for example. The small distance between the starting point and the goal is then traversed in many varied ways with the whole group of children. There is no need for the adult to give very much of an explanation beforehand, but only lead by example. Here are a few suggestions:

· Walk normally, there and back
· Walk with your "seven-mile-boots" (take the largest steps possible)
· Hop like a frog
· Two children hold both of each other's hands and run sideways
· Hop on either one or both feet
· Walk with goose feet; that is, one foot directly in front of the other

It should be understood that we do not correct the children in any way. Every child should be allowed to emulate the adult's movements without inhibition, according to his or her own ability, with the greatest joy and enthusiasm.

Tag is a familiar version of "Chase and Catch." School children from the first grade on play tag with very specific rules. For example: first a counting verse is used to determine who is "it." Then all the others run off and the person playing "it" has to try and tag any other person. The person who was tagged is now "it" and has to try and tag someone else. In this way the person doing the chasing constantly changes. However, everyone has to pay attention so they know who is "it" and can quickly run out of the way.

   Before the game begins, there may be one or more areas designated as "safe" places where the runners are allowed to rest for a moment without being tagged; trees or house corners, for instance.

Little Tree, Switch

This game requires a few trees that are standing not too far apart. The children stand by the trees in groups of two, three or more. An adult stands in the middle of the group of trees and shouts:

Little tree, little tree, switch!

Then all the children leave their trees and run to one of the other trees.

The adult also runs to another tree, because perhaps one or two children have already joyfully run to her place to shout:

Little tree, little tree, switch!

They do not yet understand that the object of the game is to find their own tree. You should absolutely let them play the game in this harmless, fun way.

With school-age children (first through third grade) you should stick to the established rules. That means, with a larger group of children, you first agree whether just one child or a group of children will be allowed to stand by each tree. One child will stand in the middle of the group of trees. After she has shouted "little tree, little tree, switch," she runs to find another tree right away.

Whoever does not find a tree is the next one to stand in the middle. The object of the game is to always find a tree and not have to stand in the middle.

If there are more trees than children, then you should mark the trees to be used in the game. For instance, you could tie a jump rope around a tree to mark it.

"Rabbit Hutch" is a good variation of this game if there are no trees are around. Use wooden hoops or strings tied into a circle and place them on the ground. Inside every hoop or string-circle sit one or more children as the rabbits. One child stands in the middle and calls:

Bunny child, run away, free and wild!

Everyone jumps out of the circles and looks for another one. Whoever cannot find an empty "hutch" has to be the caller next time.

Little Horse Game

A very nice game with many possible variations is created when children put on "horse reins." That means, one child is the coachman and another child plays the horse. The "horse" has to trot, run or stand still exactly as the coachman directs. Sometimes a coachman might have two or even three horses with which he joyfully runs around the yard. "Horses" are not allowed to run around without reins.

A six-foot-long strap simply tied into a circle can serve as the reins. First we put the circle around the child's waist and then pull one end over the head and behind the neck. The straps extend down and under the arms, like the straps of a backpack. That way there is no chance of an accident.

Hide and Seek

If there are a few trees and bushes in the landscape, a kindergarten group can play hide and seek. However, the group should not consist mainly of three- and four-year-olds.

One of the older children stands by a tree, closes her eyes and loudly recites the following verse two times:

One, two, three, four, run around,
Everyone hide so you can't be found,
Not behind me, that won't do…
One, two, three, here I come!

During the verse everyone runs to find a hiding place. The five- and six-year-olds already understand well enough how to really hide and they wait patiently to be found. Naturally, some will peek out now and then to call attention to their hiding place or to see where the seeker is. The younger children will often "hide" by simply sitting behind a tree or under a bush with one or two other children; or even by standing facing a tree. Their favorite thing is to hide with an adult, as long as he does not happen to be the seeker.

At the end of the verse, which should not be spoken too quickly, the seeker sets out to look in one hiding place after the other.

There is a joyful reunion each time someone is found and they join with the seeker until everyone has been found. Then the game begins all over again.

If you have a group of children made up of mostly five- and six-year-olds the game could be played with the familiar rules. For instance, you could have the rule that the seeker must declare each "found" person "out" by running to the starting point and saying (for example): "I see Kathrin; she's out." If the "found" person reaches the starting point before the seeker, he can declare himself free. We have to make sure that the rules are followed exactly with school children in the first grade and up; which means, for instance, that anyone declared "out" has to remain at the starting point and is "caught," but whoever reaches the starting point before the seeker is "free." Either the first or last person to be caught by the seeker has to be the seeker in the next game. If the seeker is not able to catch anyone then she has to be the seeker again.

Cat and Mouse

Melody: A. Künstler

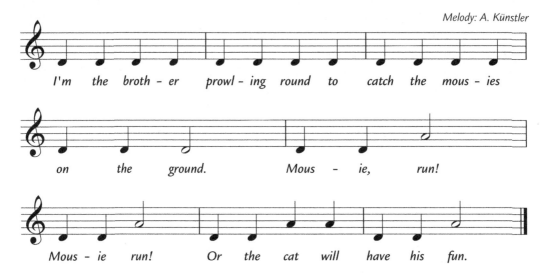

I'm the broth - er prowl - ing round to catch the mous - ies

on the ground. Mous - ie, run!

Mous - ie run! Or the cat will have his fun.

The children hold hands and, together with an adult, form a circle. One child sits in the middle as the little mouse. Another child walks around the outside of the circle as the cat, for as long as the song lasts.

Now, the cat tries to catch the mouse by attempting to get inside the circle. At the same time, the mouse runs out of the circle. When the mouse is caught, two more children are chosen to be the cat and mouse.

With a mixed-age group (three to six years old) it is advisable to have two children of the same age play the cat and mouse. Three- or four-year-olds usually very quickly run into each other's arms, while the older children can really enjoy the game by using tactics such as quick changes in direction and fast reaction times.

If this game is played with five- to eight-year-olds, you could agree that the mouse will always be helped but the cat will always be hindered; the children holding hands in the circle would raise their arms for the mouse and quickly lower them again when the cat tries to get through.

Kling, Klang, Gloria

Melody: A. Künstler

The children stand in a circle, holding hands. Two children sit in the middle. They are princesses and could be wearing a yellow cloth. Two children stand outside the circle. They are princes and could be wearing a red cloth.

The circle begins to move clockwise while singing the above song. The two princes hold hands and walk counterclockwise around the outside of the circle.

With the words "First stone, second stone, third stone. . ." the circle stops moving and one prince takes three children in a row out of the circle and these children must now walk with the princes. This is repeated until all the children have been taken out of the circle and the princesses are free.

Now the two princes go into the middle of the circle and dance with the princesses. The other children dance around them. You could choose the following song for dancing, for example:

Melody: Freya Jaffke

Come, let's all be danc - ing, danc - ing, danc - ing,

Clap - ping with our hands, Hi - ya - ya,

Clap - ping with our hands.

In the third and fifth bars in subsequent stanzas:

Stamping with our feet,
Swimming like a fish,
Flying like a bird,
Hopping like a frog,
And we all hold hands,

Or:

And we all stand still.

Everyone stands in a large, loosely formed circle. Do the following with the song:

· Bars 1 and 2: With right hand extended as invitation to dance, circle each other one time.
· Bars 3 and 5: Do the corresponding movements while standing.
· Bar 4: Always clap.

If it is a small group consisting mainly of children older than five, you could have only two children play the prince and princess, instead of four. You could also agree to take only one child out of the circle at a time.

Naturally, this game could also be played indoors very easily.

Fisher, Fisher, How Deep Is the Water?

The children stand in a loosely formed row or group opposite the adult (the first "fisher"), who stands at least thirteen to sixteen feet away. The following dialogue takes place between the fisher and the children:

Children: Fisher, fisher, how deep is the water?
Fisher: [for example] A hundred feet deep!
Children: How do we cross?
Fisher: [for example] Like fish!

Holding arms and hands in front of the body, the "fish" indicate the undulating motion of swimming fish and go towards the fisher. Other possible movements:

· Like frogs: Crouch and hop
· Like birds: "Fly over the water," with arms outstretched
· Like ducks: paddle with the hands to the right and left of the body; very small steps.
· Like storks: wade across, raising the knees very high with each step.

After everyone has reached the fisher the game begins again, but first a new fisher has to be chosen. With this game it should probably be one of the older children.

Mother, May I Travel?

A few children stand in a row next to each other. Opposite them, at a distance of about sixteen to thirty-two feet, is the adult (playing "Mother"). Using the following small dialogue, the adult chooses names of cities or countries which are already somewhat familiar to the children. The child standing on the end of the row begins:

Child: Mother, may I travel?
Mother: Yes!
Child: To where?
Mother: To Boston! [for example]

The child repeats the name of the city while walking a few steps toward the mother. Then that child stops and it is the next child's turn to ask.

Some of the five- and six-year-olds will already understand to step the exact number of syllables; two steps for "Bos-ton," for instance. The younger children often will simply walk as long as they are speaking and you should absolutely let them do that. For instance, a child may repeat "to Boston" and then take two to five steps.

After all the children have had a turn it starts over again with the first child. It is easy to measure out the distance to the adult by choosing shorter or longer place names. After most of the children have arrived where the adult is standing the game begins again. If more than five to eight children wish to play you could also have two children travel at once; otherwise the waiting period becomes too long.

With school children from first grade on we would of course pay attention that they step the exact number of syllables. But this rule applies to them also: the first to arrive at "Mother's" place may then play the mother and everyone else has to return to the starting place. Naturally, for this reason, most children try to take steps as big as they possibly can.

A variation of this game is that you direct the children to walk in a certain way. In that case, the dialogue would go like this:

Child: Mother, may I travel?
Mother: Yes!
Child: How many steps?
Mother: Ten goose steps!

Perform the "goose steps" by placing one foot directly in front of the other. Or one may ask for a certain number of giant steps (very large steps), gnome steps (normal, small steps), chicken feet (a half-step), and so on.

Games for Developing Motor Skills

Jumping Rope

Jumping rope is a well-loved activity for children. The best way for them to learn is through imitation whereby the younger children learn from the older ones. Even three- to four-year-olds will occasionally want to jump rope. They hold the rope very tightly and jump (although not rhythmically) and then bring the rope over their head and walk over it. They are not able to master the coordination needed to complete both movements together. Four- to five-year-olds are already able to bring the rope around and jump over it once or twice. Five- and six-year-olds find real joy in practicing. They are soon able to step-jump as well as jump with both feet together. A few are even able to get in a double jump.

It is a special joy to have a really long jump rope. One end should be tied to a tree or a stair banister so that only one adult is needed to turn the rope. In this way it is possible to adjust the motion according to each child's individual jumping rhythm (or lack of rhythm). At first, three- and four-year-olds only jump from side to side over the rope which is held just very slightly above the ground. Each of the older children will have their own tempo, intervals between jumps, and height of jumps. Being able to watch the six-year-olds is a big help to the younger ones, who unconsciously absorb the elders' consistent rhythm. The children will find their own rhythm through repeated, joyful practice.

It is best to wait to introduce songs and rhymes until some kind of consistent jumping rhythm has been achieved. But then rhythmic speaking or singing is a big help and is also very nice for the children who are watching.

Here are some examples:

Dance, dance, Gretel girl,
With your fine, pretty shoes!
Lift your feet as fast as you dare,
'Til the wind blows through your hair.
Dance, dance, Gretel girl,
With your fine, pretty shoes.

Dance, dance, Hansel boy,
With your fine, pointy cap!
You have to catch me, oh so quick,
Don't stand there like a lolly stick!
Dance, dance, Hansel boy,
With your fine, pointy cap!

—from Thüringen

Children from the first grade on who already know how to jump rope often find great happiness in this activity. They display perseverance with it and challenge themselves in increasingly difficult ways.

They are soon able to jump in and out without missing a beat, while two people are turning a long jump rope. They will also try to run through without jumping. An older child or an adult should show them once how it is done and then it is only a question of having the courage to do it.

Now it is also possible for two or three children to jump rope at the same time if the rope is long enough.

Games Using a Ball

Even the youngest children are happy playing with a ball. As soon as they are able to walk they will roll a ball away from them and run after it. Three-year-olds are already able to have a ball thrown to them from a very short distance, catch it and throw it back. The older and more dexterous they become the greater the distance they can throw and certain challenges can be introduced, such as throwing the ball in the air and catching it again; throwing a ball very high in the air and letting an adult catch it; bouncing a ball on the floor and catching it again; throwing a ball backwards through the legs, and so on.

The main thing is that the children are able to open themselves up trustingly as the ball comes towards them, and to catch it in their arms without shying away from it. They are learning to catch the ball without fear.

From the beginning, we should gently get the children used to grasping the ball with their hands and not kicking it away with their feet. Adults should also set an example. Catching a rolling ball will require constant bending down, but from a medical standpoint and especially for children, it is a very beneficial form of unconscious physical

training. The gesture of pushing something away with the foot also can be
easily carried over to other things that
should not be kicked, like toys that are
to be put away, for example, or sometimes even playmates.

Ball Over a Rope

We span a rope between two trees—"as
high as you can!" cry the six-year-olds.
The children stand on either side of the
rope and throw the ball to each other.
   While the older children are usually
successful in catching the ball thrown
over the rope, the younger ones are
happy if the ball just flies high in the air.
Sometimes you might want to span two
ropes at different heights.

Ball Through Two Hoops

Two hoops are fastened to the backs
of two chairs so that the hoops meet in
between, overlapping by half. The three
resulting openings create different pos-
sibilities for rolling or throwing the ball
through the hoops. We could also begin
with just one hoop and increase the level
of difficulty by increasing the distance of
the thrower from the hoop.

Ring the Bell in the Hoop

We fasten a hoop onto a stand or hang it on a tree branch or clothesline. A bell is hung from the top of the hoop, reaching the middle. From an appropriate distance, a child tries to hit the bell with the ball.

Ball in the Basket

We place a basket on top of some stacked boxes or a ladder. The ball is thrown into the basket. If the basket is large enough and the balls are on the small side, it should be possible for several children to throw balls at the same time.

An adult retrieves the balls from the basket only after all of them have landed in it.

One, Two, Three, Who Has the Ball?

One child stands in front of a row of children a little distance away, with her back to the others. She throws the ball backwards over her head where it is caught by one of the other children and hidden behind his back. When all the children are standing side by side with their hands behind their back they say: "One, two, three, who has the ball?"

The child who threw the ball turns around and has to guess. If she guesses correctly she may throw the ball again, but if not, then the child who caught the ball may go to the front.

Catch the Ball

1. The children stand in a circle and toss the ball around so that every other child gets the ball. Or, the ball is thrown diagonally across the circle.

2. Two children stand opposite each other a little distance apart and throw the ball to each other. A third child stands in the middle between them and tries to catch the ball. Or, it could also be that the two on the end try to hit the child in the middle with the ball while that child tries to avoid it.

3. The one who will begin the game is chosen by a counting verse. He throws the ball in the air and calls out the name of one of the other children. Everyone else quickly runs away until the named person has the ball in her hands and shouts: "Stop!" Everyone has to immediately stand still. The one who caught the ball now has to try to hit one of the other players with the ball. If she is successful the one who was hit has to start the game over again by throwing the ball in the air and calling out another name. If she is unsuccessful then she has another turn or simply passes the ball to the next person.

Six- to eight-year-olds like to make up their own rules for games involving balls. They have experienced older children playing these games and so they confidently use the remembered rules and make up some of their own along the way. The only important thing is that all of the children stick to the agreed-upon rules.

Can Toss

Ten same-sized cans are arranged in a pyramid on a wooden stand. The cans could have colorfully painted paper glued to them. From a marked distance, the children try to hit the pyramid with a soft ball and make as many cans as possible fall down.

Rolling Hoops

Rolling a hoop gives children completely different opportunities for training their motor skills than playing with a ball or jump rope. It is best to get the children accustomed to using a stick, approximately 8 to 10 inches long, to roll the hoop. Smooth surfaces such as park walkways are ideal for this activity.

It is best if an adult stands behind a child in the beginning while he is learning. She puts one finger of the left hand on the hoop next to the child's hand and uses her right hand to guide the child's other hand as he rolls the hoop. If we always make sure to help them start correctly, hoop-rolling will be much easier for children.

The hoop always falls down a lot in the beginning. But as soon as it gets rolling we run alongside it. Once the hoop is finally rolling we are able to guide it in different directions by quickly letting the stick slide along one side of the hoop or the other.

Five- and six-year-olds who have tried rolling the hoop a few times usually become quite good at it. They experience increasing satisfaction and happiness when they are able to keep the hoop rolling over a longer distance. Their ability to coordinate the actions of running and rolling and guiding the hoop increases more and more, and they are increasingly able to tune into the process and adapt accordingly.

Balancing

Every healthy child has a strong need to try and balance at every opportunity that presents itself. It is a way of continuing, at a higher level, that great experience of finding one's balance when learning to walk. If we have enough wide and narrow boards on hand, along with several tree stumps of varying heights, then the children will always have new ideas for how they can practice balancing. They will even use ropes laid on the ground and they especially like to do this barefoot.

In a mixed-age group it is wonderful to experience how the older children, with confidence and empathy, will offer help to the younger ones or build something easier for them to navigate.

Balancing is also something that is very easily incorporated into an obstacle course at a summer party (see p. 66).

Walking on Stilts

Walking on stilts presents a still greater challenge when it comes to finding one's balance. The younger children like to test their skills on the block stilts, which are made from round or rectangular wooden blocks with string run through them. If the rectangular blocks are finished off with a slightly rounded tread surface it increases the level of difficulty. See Freya Jaffke's book *Spielzeug von Eltern selbst gemacht* ("Toys for Parents to Make"), Stuttgart 2007.

From around age five children also like to use the familiar pole stilts. The pole stilts are usually adjustable for height. The first thing is to practice mounting the stilts by leaning your back against a wall or tree. This should be practiced before trying to take the first steps. What matters here is always being open to new challenges and practicing. It is comparable to children learning to stand for the first time; they do not become discouraged when they are not successful right away.

Six-year-olds who have already mastered walking on stilts will often look for things to do that are more difficult, like stepping over a rope that is suspended between two blocks of wood; or even walking up and down stairs.

Party Games

Introduction

The following games could be used to add something special to the daily kindergarten routine. They are also well-suited to children's parties. If there is a party involved the games will need careful preparation. This can easily be done with the children present, who will help wherever possible with eagerness and growing anticipation. This also helps them gain new impulses for their own daily play. Some of the games using a ball are also very appropriate for summer parties, for instance: "Ring the Bell" (p. 58), "Ball in the Basket" (p. 59), or "Through Two Hoops" (p. 57).

The main concern while playing these games with a group of mixed-age kindergartners is that the children have fun. The children's attention should never be drawn into comparisons with others or a sense of competiveness. For this reason we always give everyone the same thing if prizes are handed out with the games.

The way the games are played is very different if you have a group of schoolchildren age seven and older (see suggestions given at the end of each game description). Contests and the desire to win have their place with older children. However, that does not mean that the winners should get prizes every time. The fun of playing a game involving motor skills and of accomplishing something together, rather than the expectation of a prize, should always be in the foreground.

If prizes are given for one or another of the games then we should make sure that by the end every child has gotten a prize, taking into consideration that all the children have made their best efforts according to their own abilities.

Adventure Trail Obstacle Course

With boards, tree stumps and logs, tables, benches, stools and many other objects it is possible to build a course that offers a variety of experiences and activities: balancing, climbing, jumping down, crawling through, aiming (with a ball, for instance) or crossing a "river" (pieces of board or flat rocks are arranged on a blue cloth to be used as stepping stones). There could even be a slide (a smooth board or bench propped up, with folded towels or flat cushions at the bottom for the children to land on).

Everyone can create such an obstacle course according to their abilities, even indoors.

Naturally, we will accompany the younger children along the entire course and may even need to take their hand. In any case, there should always be an adult standing by the slide and also supervising ball-throwing activities.

If you have a group of five- to six-year-olds such an adventure trail could be combined with a story. Perhaps at the end there is a treasure to be discovered.

One fun example of "treasure" given at the end of the obstacle course would be little wood-bark boats and "helmsmen," described in the following section, to be sailed in large buckets or tubs filled with water.

Simple Boats

First, make a boat from wood bark. Find or fashion an oval-shaped piece of bark, about two to three inches long, and a small stick for the mast, about 2 ½ inches long. Drill a hole in the bark and put the little stick through the hole. Cut a cloth sail into a triangle or trapezoidal shape and glue it to the mast.

Now make the helmsman. Cut a 2 ½-inch square from a piece of thin, solid-colored fabric. Using wool or cotton, shape a pea-sized ball for the head and place it at the center of the square. Tie the "neck" with thread. The rest of the fabric forming the body is trimmed at the bottom so the "helmsman" is able to stand. It should be about 1 ½ inches tall.

You may also make boats out of nutshells. Scrape out the nut-meat from half a walnut shell. Drop or press a pea-sized bit of beeswax into the middle of the shell. Place a matchstick in the beeswax for the mast, and add a small sail. It is perfectly fine to have only one "helmsman" in the boat.

During Advent a tiny, burning candle could be attached to the nutshell. In a regatta, the winner would the one whose candle did not go out. A good prize would be a little boat or a pretty shell.

A little wooden boat can be made beginning with a piece of a branch that is about seven inches long with a diameter of three to four inches. Saw it in half lengthwise. The curve on the bottom is flattened out with a wood plane or chisel so the boat can sit flat without tipping. Carve the form of the boat with a hand knife or pocketknife. Use a gouging tool to hollow out the boat as much as needed for it to hold a cargo. Round off the edges with a knife or sandpaper. Bore a hole in the middle for the mast. Glue a cloth sail onto the mast or nail on one made of birch bark.

If you do not have some kind of gouging tool you can make the boat could from a flat piece of wood or a thick piece of tree bark. Glue or screw on a very small basket or wooden bowl to hold the cargo.

Blow the Little Boat

A tub in the yard filled with water in the middle of summer is sure to attract children who would like to sail these little boats. A little bit of "wind" blown carefully on the sail should make the boat go without tipping it.

We could build a lighthouse in the middle of the "sea" for older children by simply propping a thick, round branch between two big rocks in the bottom of the tub, so that the branch sticks up out of the water like a lighthouse.

A starting point for a regatta could be marked on the edge of the tub. The children race by blowing their little boats one time around the lighthouse. The winner is the one whose helmsman wasn't lost or whose boat did not overturn.

For a summer party we put a blue cloth on the bottom of the tub and scatter some colorful rocks and shells over it so they can be seen through the clear water.

Pull the Little Boat

Two or three children sit next to each other on a bench or log. The game could take place on the grass, sandy ground or indoors. Each child holds a small round wooden peg (about four inches long and two inches in diameter) with a string tied to it that is about six to ten feet long. The boat is fastened to the other end of the string. There is a little doll or a small cargo in the boat (for parties the cargo could be a strawberry or apricot, for example). The children begin to wind up the string on the peg thereby slowly pulling the boat closer to them. After the boat arrives the cargo is unloaded. Then the string is unwound for the next child.

71

This game is very peaceful and contemplative and the children should never be hurried.

Schoolchildren from the first grade and up could have a contest pulling their boats. It is important to make sure that all the boats are equally good, all the wooden pegs have the same diameter and the strings are all the same length.

An adult should give the start signal. You could have rules such as: any boat that loses its cargo has to stop and wait until it is loaded again.

A second round could be played in which first all the losers have a contest among themselves, then a third round for the winners to compete, and so on.

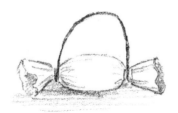

Fishing

A large, blue cloth is spread on the ground for the lake. Some wood pieces or other objects could be laid underneath to give the appearance of waves. The "lake" could be bordered all around with rocks, wood, or shells. Colorful rocks, various shells and "little fish" are scattered on the top.

The children take the fishing poles and quietly fish until they have caught one or two. Three- and four-year-old children usually still have difficulty catching a fish. They like to take the hook in the other hand and then try to catch the fish from a much closer distance. You could also help them a little with guiding the pole. The older children should just be left to try on their own even if it takes a little longer. Anxious or restless children are usually very quiet for a few moments while fishing.

This game can easily be played indoors as well.

Make the fishing pole from a line fastened onto a stick 12 to 14 inches long. Attach a piece of thick wire bent into a hook.

We mold all kinds of "fish" for everyday use out of colorful beeswax and press metal rings about one inch in diameter into them (see drawing at left). For parties we make

fish out of something edible. You could use small fruits, nuts, dates, etc. You wrap them in foil, for instance, and simply twist the ends like a candy wrapper. You can fashion handles to both ends of the wrapper using florist's wire, making it easier to hook the "fish." Make sure the wire handle is not too small; it should be about 2 to2 ¼ inches in diameter.

When the fish are put in the lake make sure the wire handles are sticking straight up. A basket is sitting next to the lake to hold the wrappings left after children snack on their "catch."

Ring Toss

The first thing we do is make rings out of something like willow or hazel rods. Young shoots cut in early summer work best, soaked in a tub of water for a few days to make them more pliable.

Form the rods into rings with a diameter of about eight to ten inches. You can do this in a number of ways: for example, wrapping the ends around the ring two or three times, or overlapping the ends and wrapping them with string. As long as the rods are still damp we are able to shape the rings into a nice circle. The rings could also be made out of very tightly braided twine.

Now we put a few sticks in the ground. The sticks should show at least 12-20 inches above the ground. From an agreed-upon distance, marked for instance by a string laid on the ground or the edge of the sandbox, the children now try to toss the rings over the sticks.

Marbles in the Lake

We take a flat bowl (an old plate or a flat enamel pan would also work) and put it in a depression in the sand so that the edge of the bowl is even with the ground.

Either with a string or a line in the sand we mark out a circle about three feet away from the bowl. The children will squat or kneel behind this circle. Each child gets a few marbles which they try to roll into the "lake."

Marbles that get stuck may only be retrieved after all the other marbles have been rolled out. It is best if an adult gathers the marbles and hands them out again.

Older children quickly develop a sense for how much force they need to roll the marbles all the way to the lake. Some children are too cautious at first, but then overjoyed when a marble lands in the lake. The more energetic children sometimes overshoot the lake completely.

About the Author

Freya Jaffke is a master Steiner/Waldorf kindergarten teacher and teacher trainer from Germany who has lectured and offered workshops for educators and parents in many countries. Her books on early childhood have sold over a quarter of a million copies worldwide, including *Toymaking with Children*, *Magic Wool, Celebrating Festivals with Children*, and *Work and Play in Early Childhood* (all Floris Books). WECAN plans to publish a new English translation of her book of songs and singing games, *Let's Dance and Sing*.

She also edited and compiled *On the Play of the Child: Rudolf Steiner's Indications for Working with Young Children*, which was prepared as study material for the 2005 international Waldorf early childhood educators' conference. WECAN published the first English edition in 2006, and a second, revised and expanded edition in 2012.

Now retired, she continues to be active with marionette plays and teaching crafts and doll making at the Nikolas Cusanus House near Stuttgart.

Made in the USA
Columbia, SC
28 December 2021

52923713R00046